PAINT IT

Dek Messecar

Series Consultant Editor: Bob Tattersall

CONTENTS

COLLINS

Introduction

Painting is the least expensive and the easiest way to change or brighten up your home, and today's paints offer a wide variety of colours and finishes from which to choose.

This book explains, clearly and simply, how to tackle household painting jobs. With a little patience, practice, and a methodical approach, anyone can paint the interior of their home. For the more ambitious, there are full instructions on how to do your exterior painting as well.

The main body of the book is divided into two sections: one for inside and one for outside painting. There is also information on the tools and materials you'll need, and advice on ladders, steps, scaffolding and safety.

The point to be stressed with all the jobs described in this book is the importance of preparation. Flaws in surfaces are accentuated by coats of paint rather than hidden by them. Remember that no painted finish can be any smoother than the surface to which it is applied.

Another important point is that manufacturers' instructions and recommendations sometimes vary between brands, even for quite similar products. If in doubt, always follow the manufacturers' instructions.

Above *Buttercup yellow and white gloss were selected for this small kitchen. The same yellow is echoed in the blind, giving a sunny feel. Reflections in the gloss help create an illusion of space.*

Above right *A dramatic effect, created by painting the entire front of this Edwardian house a dark brown, also disguises ugly pipes. The windows and porch have been picked out in white, along with the eaves and lintels.*

Right *A cool and restful choice of colour scheme enhances this elegant room. The ceiling and walls are painted in light blue, with cornice, woodwork and unused fireplace all picked out in white silk.*

TOOLS AND MATERIALS

Brushes
Good brushes are essential for good results and, with proper maintenance, will last for years. Buy the size you need for each job when you are buying the paint so that you build up a complete set, say 10mm, 25mm, 50mm, 75mm, and 150mm wide. The best brushes have natural bristles that are significantly longer than those of cheaper ones. They also have more bristles per brush and have a firmer 'spring' when you flex them. There are two specialized brushes that will prove useful:

The *cutting-in brush* is trimmed at a slight angle and is invaluable for painting straight lines, up to corners, glazing bars of window frames, and all awkward edges.

The *radiator brush* (or crevice brush) is used to get paint to parts of the wall covered by radiators or perhaps by a large object too difficult to move.

Care and Cleaning
New brushes should be washed in water and a little washing up liquid and allowed to dry before using them for the first time; this helps remove loose hairs. When dry, flex the bristles back and forth vigorously between thumb and finger.

To work properly, the bristles must be free to slide against each other. When paint has worked its way to the top of the bristles, the brush is 'bound up' and the only remedy is to clean and dry it. Have second one handy when painting.

To clean brushes, get off as much of the paint as you can by using the brush on plenty of newspaper. Then, if it is *oil-based paint*, choose a container just large enough to hold the brush and pour in enough white spirit or proprietary brush cleaner to cover the bristles completely. Plunge the brush up and down vigorously.

Run a wire brush through the bristles from handle to

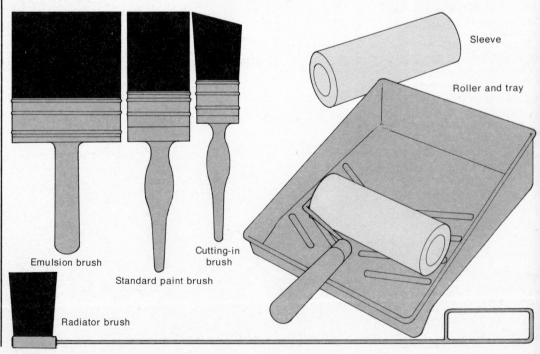

Emulsion brush

Standard paint brush

Cutting-in brush

Radiator brush

Sleeve

Roller and tray

tip on each side to remove any paint that is too dry to dissolve easily. Change the white spirit and repeat.

Wash the brush in warm water and a little washing up liquid. Rinse in clean water. Repeat the process, rinsing several times until the bristles are free of detergent. Shake out as much water as possible, smooth the bristles into shape and store flat; never leave standing on the bristles.

When using oil-based paint, brushes may be stored overnight (between coats, for instance) with the bristles immersed in water. Don't immerse the metal ferrule as it may rust.

If you have been using *water-based paint*, the procedure is the same, but leave out the step with white spirit and use the wire brush during washing.

If a brush has become hardened by paint left in it, soak it in paint stripper (water soluble) or proprietary brush restorer until soft, and then clean as described above.

Rollers

Rollers are useful for painting large areas such as walls and ceilings. Buy a good quality lambswool or mohair roller, and take care of it. Generally speaking, long-pile rollers are used for rougher surfaces, such as pebbledash, and short-pile for smooth surfaces. However, different piles produce different textures on smooth surfaces with some paints.

A good roller should have an easily removable sleeve (for cleaning) and some have an extension handle for painting ceilings etc. without ladders. A tray is used to 'charge' the roller with paint. It has a sloping section on which to work the roller up and down to distribute the paint evenly.

To clean a roller, use up the paint on newspaper, remove the sleeve and immerse it in water or white spirit as appropriate. Wearing rubber gloves, rub the pile thoroughly while it is submerged. Finish by washing in lukewarm water and washing up liquid and then rinsing thoroughly. Shake off as much water as possible and leave it standing on end to dry.

Paint Pads

Paint pads are an alternative if large brushes and rollers seem too heavy. They are usually used with water-based paint on large surfaces such as walls and ceilings, but can be used with oil-based paints.

The best pads have a mohair pile on a layer of foam attached to a plastic handle. The foam is to allow the pile to follow the surface being painted, not to soak up paint; only the pile

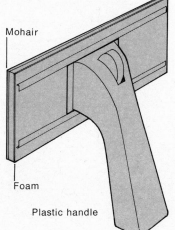

Mohair

Foam

Plastic handle

should be charged. The easiest way to avoid overloading the pad is to use a tray with a roller that picks up paint and transfers it to the pile as the pad is moved across the top of it. These trays are inexpensive and may come with the pads.

Properly loaded, paint pads leave an even film of paint with each wipe. If the paint streaks or drags, you are probably pulling the pad too quickly for the paint to spread evenly. Clean pads after use the same way as rollers.

Other Tools

Paint kettles are recommended when painting with a brush, especially from a ladder. They keep the can free of the bits and stray hairs that inevitably result from dipping the brush in it. Fill them to a depth of half the length of the bristles of the brush you're using. This helps to avoid overloading the brush.

Paint shields are flat pieces of plastic used to keep paint off window panes when painting the glazing bars. They are specially shaped to allow the paint to cover the join between putty and glass (important for weather proofing).

Paint stripper is a chemical liquid used to remove old paint. In preparation for repainting, it is more usual to use a *blowtorch* or *hot air paint remover*. This is a difficult and sometimes dangerous job and it is usually enough to scrape off unsound areas and rub down well.

Scrapers are stiff, metal-blade spatulas used for removing old wallpaper and flaking paint.

Filling knives are similar to scrapers but have flexible blades and are used to apply filler to cracks and holes in surfaces.

Abrasive paper is used to smooth surfaces before painting and also to roughen gloss paint before painting over it. Aluminium oxide paper doesn't clog easily and lasts longer than glass paper. When rubbing down between coats to make a very smooth finish, 'wet and dry' cloth-backed silicon carbide is best as it can be rinsed in water to prevent it becoming clogged with paint as you work.

Always wrap abrasive paper around a block of wood for flat surfaces. For large curves, staple the edges together to make a loop around your hand or use any object of a convenient shape as a sanding block.

When painting over old gloss paint, you can use a chemical product called *liquid sander* to prepare the surface without rubbing down.

Dust sheets will protect anything that may get splashed or dripped on. Fabric ones are best because they are absorbent, but polythene, although slippery, will do. Newspapers tend to move around when walked on or if there is a draught.

Automatic-feed brush, pad or roller machines are available. They have a reservoir for paint and use compressed gas to force it up a tube to the brush. They are quite expensive, and it is debatable whether they save as much time and effort as one may imagine.

Spray painting. There are small spray guns that use an aerosol propellant to spray paint from a jar. These are not expensive and are useful for many special effects.

Steam wallpaper strippers may be inexpensively hired and are very effective for removing stubborn wallpaper.

Paint stirring attachments for electric drills are inexpensive and save time and effort.

Don't use paint stripper to clean rollers or pads.

In case your brush gets 'bound up', have a second one handy.

Use white spirit on a lint-free cloth to remove last traces of dust before painting.

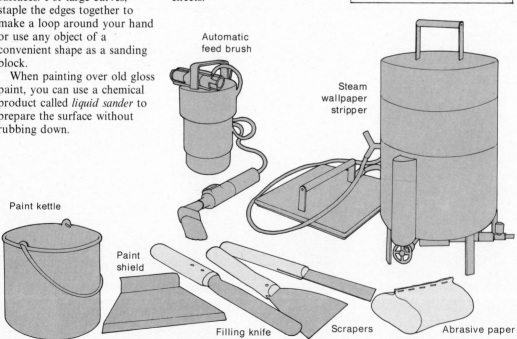

Automatic feed brush

Steam wallpaper stripper

Paint kettle

Paint shield

Filling knife

Scrapers

Abrasive paper

Types of Paint and Fillers

Paints for household decoration fall into two general categories.

Oil-based paint is thinned with white spirit and is used on wood and metal, although you can use it on walls and ceilings. It is available in matt, eggshell, and gloss finishes, although only gloss should be used for exterior painting. Oil-based paint is actually a 'system' of three different coatings: primer, undercoat and top coat. If you use a 'non-drip' top coat, apply it with a minimum of brushing and don't stir it beforehand.

Water-based paints are a vast range of emulsions for interior and exterior use on plaster, lining paper, brick and cement. Interior grades come in matt and silk finishes as well as thick resin mixtures that give texture to walls and ceilings. Exterior grades range from matt finish to masonry paints that contain granulated quartz or mica and have a sandy appearance.

Micro porous versions of both oil- and water-based paints are becoming available. These are said to be more resistant to flaking and peeling, especially on wood outside. These must be used with micro porous primers and undercoats and are not effective if used on top of old paint.

As well as conventional paint, there are specialized paints for specific purposes:

Radiator enamel is designed not to discolour with heat.

Stove paint will withstand the heat of stoves and fireplaces and comes in a range of colours.

Glass paint comes in transparent colours for a stained glass effect.

Tile red is used for roof and floor tiles and brick.

Multi-coloured paint gives a speckled effect.

Epoxy resin paint is available for floors and surfaces where durability is needed.

Matt black can make chalk boards on most smooth surfaces.

Artists acrylic paint is used for stencilling.

Damp proof paints may help overcome dampness problems in masonry, but they do not cure the causes. However, full instructions for dealing with damp come with these products.

Bitumen (tar) paint is for waterproofing the inside of gutters.

Knotting is a coating applied to knots in wood before applying primer or paint. Otherwise, resin from the knot will bleed through later. There are proprietary products or you can use shellac.

Thinners are simply the appropriate solvent for each type of paint. Instructions on the can almost always state whether the paint should be thinned and what to use for brush cleaning.

Primer is a coating used to take up absorbency and give a uniform surface to paint on.

Undercoat is used under oil-based paint to give an opaque colour and good surface.

Primer/sealer is an oil-based primer used to bind surfaces and stop old paint colours or wallpaper bleeding through.

Masonry sealer is a primer for brick and cement.

Wood preservative is a product for protecting exterior wood from rot and decay.

Universal stainers are tubes of coloured pigment that can be used with most types of paint to mix your own colours.

Filler is the term given to materials used to repair cracks or depressions in wood, plaster or metal.

For wood and plaster, the best fillers are resin based, sold as powder to be mixed with water or already mixed. These are hard, smooth, easy to rub down when dry, and also have the advantage of not shrinking as they harden. This means they can be applied flush with the surface, not proud as with cellulose filler.

Large areas of damaged plaster should be repaired with plaster or one of the DIY plastering systems that is applied by brush and remains soft long enough to give several attempts at smoothing it.

Metal should be filled with a two-part resin filler of the type used to repair car bodywork.

Mastic is an oil-based filler used to seal joins in exterior wood against moisture.

Using Steps and Ladders Safely

Indoors

Before tackling the painting job you have in mind, you should give some thought to the problem of reaching it. Time spent making good arrangements to reach the work can mean the difference between a satisfying job and a frustrating (and dangerous) experience.

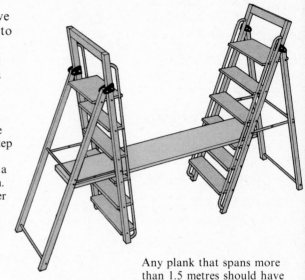

Low walls and ceilings require only a small set of steps or step ladder. For *high walls and ceilings* two step ladders and a plank make a better platform. This speeds the work as larger sections can be covered.

Stairs present a complication. It is possible to hire purpose-built ladder systems for stairs, or you can use an arrangement of long ladder, step ladder and planks.

Any plank that spans more than 1.5 metres should have another plank secured on the top of it.

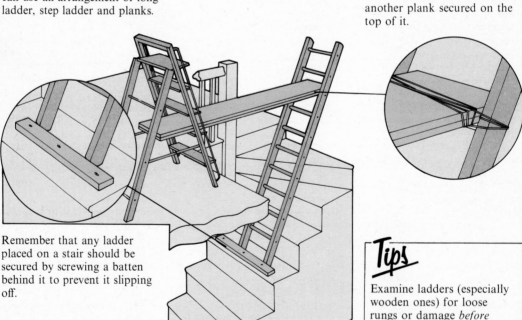

Remember that any ladder placed on a stair should be secured by screwing a batten behind it to prevent it slipping off.

Tips

Examine ladders (especially wooden ones) for loose rungs or damage *before* using them.

Don't stand too high on a ladder. Keep your waist below the top rung.

Outdoors

You will probably need extending ladders and possibly scaffolding. These are readily available for hire and are not expensive. Even if you are considering buying your own, it is a good idea to hire first so you can be sure of buying the right type. One point to note is that aluminium ladders are far easier to handle than wooden ones. Examine the ground where you will erect your ladders or scaffolding *before* you hire, as some systems can make allowance for unevenness and others cannot.

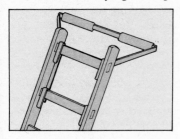

A *ladder stay* is useful on high walls, both to steady the ladder and give more area to work on.

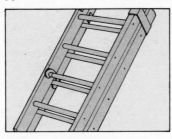

Extending ladders should never overlap less than four rungs when extended.

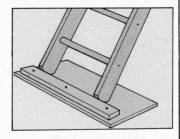

On soft ground, secure the ladder on a board with a batten fixed behind.

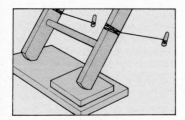

Long ladders must be secured at the bottom by rope or batten. On uneven ground, make a level base by using well-secured blocks or planks.

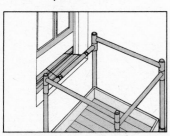

Scaffolding towers must be secured to the building near the top to prevent them from toppling over.

Erect extending ladders by placing the foot against the bottom of the wall and 'walking' it up. Then extend the ladder and pull the foot away from the wall $\frac{1}{4}$ of the height.

INTERIOR PAINTING

Colour and texture can be used to enhance or subdue features of a room. A low ceiling can be 'raised' by painting it one or two shades lighter than the walls. A high ceiling will appear lower if painted a dark tone. In the same way that colours appear lighter as the area increases, light colours increase the apparent size of the area they cover. To help balance a long narrow space, contrast the light colours of the small walls with significantly darker long walls. Highlighting picture rails or cornices can help the proportions of a tall room, while contrasting colours on the woodwork will seem to bring the walls closer in a large low-ceilinged room.

Choosing colours by using colour charts is unreliable, as it is difficult to know how the colour will be affected by the light and size of the surface to which it is applied. The best solution is to test some paint on a small area.

Mixing your own colours with tubes of pigment and base colour of paint allows you to experiment in this way. The main thing is to remember how much of which pigments you have added to each sample (writing in pencil on the wall is convenient) and to let the samples dry before making the final choice.

Ready-mixed colours. Buy the smallest can available and use it on a test area. Some manufacturers supply very small samples for this purpose. They are inexpensive and the price may be refunded when buying the full-size cans.

With all ready-mixed colours, you should buy at least enough for the job as there is often some variation between batches. It is also important to stir thoroughly unless the manufacturers' instructions specifically forbid it.

Left See how contrast between woodwork and walls can bring out detail that would be lost in a single-colour scheme. This staircase has become a sharply defined feature, rather than merging with the wall.

Right A mural in matt and silk finish water-based paint. Designs should be marked out in pencil after painting background colours. Use a straight edge or chalk line for straight lines, and a pencil tied to string for uniform curves. A cutting-in brush is invaluable for this kind of detail. Apply the paint as heavily as possible to keep the number of coats to a minimum.

Colours mixed in the paint shop have a nasty habit of holding a concentrated area of pigment in the can.

Types of paint. Traditionally, oil-based paint has been used on wood and metal, and emulsion paint on plaster and lining paper. This generally holds true with the modern synthetic versions of these types of paint. Emulsions have largely been replaced by vinyl based and latex based paints, which are more washable and in some cases may be used on wood. Oil-based paints have been replaced by several synthetics (such as alkyd) and are generally more hard wearing and long-lasting as well as being more expensive. However, both traditional types are still available. Detailed descriptions of the suitability of any paint for particular surfaces and the correct solvent for thinning and brush cleaning usually appear on the can.

Textures. A major advantage of the wide choice of paints today is the various textures that can be applied to any surface. Paints for wood are available in gloss, silk or eggshell, and matt finish. Paints for walls and ceilings come in these finishes, and also as thick resin mixtures to be stippled or trowelled on, or used with a patterned roller to give a rough plaster effect.

This textured paint has the advantage of covering small cracks and imperfections with a minimum of preparation. You should remember, however, that the surface must be sound enough to accept the paint, and that once on, it is very difficult to remove, stipples and all. It can be overpainted and damaged portions can be touched up, so it is best regarded as permanent, once applied.

Preparing Walls and Ceilings

The first step is to assess the state of the walls and ceiling. Although no longer common, there could be *whitewash* or *distemper* on them. The way to find out is to scrub an area with warm water to see if the colour comes off and the bare plaster is reached. If it does, you must wash off as much as possible and apply a coat of oil based primer/sealer to the whole surface.

If there is *wallpaper* it is best to remove it. However, if the paper is in good condition or has been overpainted already, you may prefer to leave it on. But this does not apply to vinyl wall coverings which must be peeled off and the backing paper removed in the normal way as described below.

Wallpaper

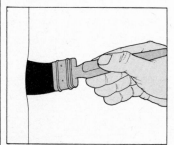

Repair any loose edges with wallpaper paste.

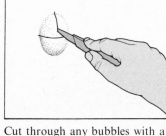

Cut through any bubbles with a sharp blade.

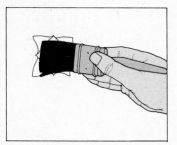

Paste under the flaps and stick them down.

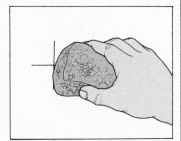

Remove any excess paste from the surface. Leave paper to dry.

Removing wallpaper
Score the surface of the paper with a stiff wire brush. Using a large paintbrush, soak the paper with warm water containing a little vinegar. Scrape off with a stiff scraping knife, being careful not to dig into the wall. Work on a large area and keep re-soaking until the paper comes off easily, leaving little residue. For stubborn paper, hire a steam stripper. Wash off all traces of old paste before painting.

Plaster, concrete and brick

New walls need several weeks to dry before painting. Seal plaster with primer/sealer (or a thinned coat of the paint you intend using) and seal brick and concrete with a proprietary masonry sealer. This will neutralize any alkali in the mortar that could affect the paint.

Old, unpainted concrete and brick should be washed and, when thoroughly dry, sealed with masonry sealer.

Previously painted surfaces need washing with a mild solution of household detergent and water. This must be thoroughly rinsed and allowed to dry.

Any flaking paint should be scraped back to a firm edge.

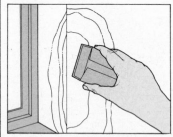

Rub the area with abrasive paper to feather the edges of the surrounding paint.

If the previous paint is gloss finish, it must be rubbed down or treated with liquid sander to key the new paint.

Filling

Now is the time to fill cracks and depressions in the surface. First, brush all dust and loose material out of the damaged area and, in the case of hairline cracks, widen them slightly with a knife as filler isn't effective for cracks less than 1mm wide. Use a flexible knife and filler as described in the Tools and Materials Section.

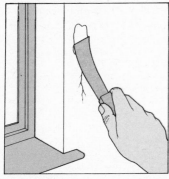

Scoop some filler on to the end of the knife and press the blade flat over the fault, sliding away to leave the filler in the hole. You may need several attempts to ensure the filler is pushed right to the bottom without air being trapped underneath.

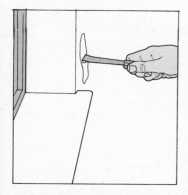

Holding the knife almost vertical, scrape across the top to remove the excess.

Professionals try to clean all the surplus away (including the ridges around the edges) leaving the repair flush. It's worth the extra time spent on the wet filler as rubbing down afterwards is messy, time consuming, and hard work.

Large, deep faults should be filled in layers 3mm thick. These will dry quickly enough for you to apply another layer every so often while dealing with the other repairs. This helps with faults that are wider than the filling knife, as the surface is built up gradually around the edges, reducing the area to be scraped off flush. Remember to clean the surplus from around the edges each time you fill.

Very large areas of damaged plaster should be repaired with plaster or one of the DIY plastering systems that is applied by brush. These are used in layers up to 3mm thick and take 24 hours to dry between coats, so, if the fault is deeper than this, use ordinary filler to build up the surface until only a thin "skim coat" is needed. The brushed-on plaster stays soft long enough to be smoothed with a plastic spreader.

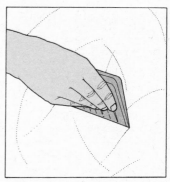

Keep working the surface (re-wetting if necessary) until you're satisfied with the finish.

To get a neat edge on outside corners, hold a polythene wrapped piece of wood against one side and flush with the edge. Then fill as if it were a crack. Carefully slide the wood away when filler begins to set.

Priming

When the filler is completely dry, rub the areas with abrasive paper to ensure they are smooth. Then all repairs and bare patches must be primed with primer/sealer or a thinned coat of paint to be used.

Seal coloured wallpapers with oil based primer/sealer or the pattern will bleed through water based paint no matter how many coats are applied.

To prevent rust stains, prime metal (nail and screw heads) with oil based primer before using filler or water based paint.

Painting Walls and Ceilings

Water-based emulsion paint

Using a brush: Choose the largest one that is comfortable to use for the large areas and a cutting-in brush for edges and corners. Stir the paint thoroughly and pour enough to fill a large paint kettle to a depth of half the length of the bristles of the large brush.

Ceilings: Start at the window end of the room. Begin in a corner and work across in a strip about 50cm wide. As one strip is completed, start from the first side again, overlapping just enough to cover evenly but not building up a ridge. Water-based paints dry quickly, and the idea is to keep the wet edge fresh enough to accept the new paint. It may help to close doors and windows to slow the drying and to paint in narrower strips.

Water-based paint can be overlapped when touch-dry, so if you have trouble keeping the edge fresh, paint large areas seperately and join them when the paint is no longer tacky. If the second coat is applied in the same way, make the joins in different places from those in the first coat to reduce shading.

If the walls are not going to be painted, use the cutting-in brush around the edge of the ceiling to make a neat join with the wall. However, if you are decorating the walls, paint over the join with the ceiling by 10mm or so to be sure there won't be any bare patches where they meet. Keep a damp cloth handy to wip any splashes off the wall.

Walls: Begin at the top corner of a wall near a window so you will be working away from the light. You can work in horizontal or vertical strips, paying particular attention to making a neat join with the ceiling. Make sure you keep the wet edge fresh.

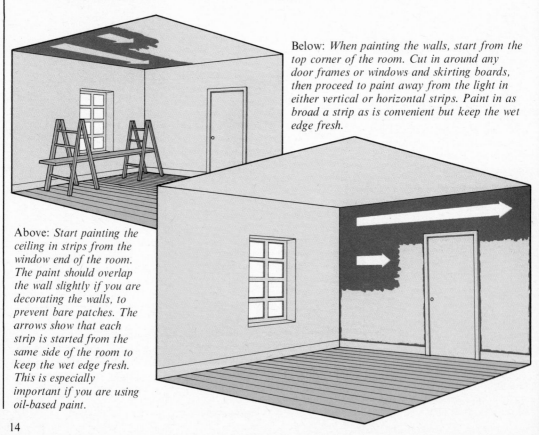

Below: *When painting the walls, start from the top corner of the room. Cut in around any door frames or windows and skirting boards, then proceed to paint away from the light in either vertical or horizontal strips. Paint in as broad a strip as is convenient but keep the wet edge fresh.*

Above: *Start painting the ceiling in strips from the window end of the room. The paint should overlap the wall slightly if you are decorating the walls, to prevent bare patches. The arrows show that each strip is started from the same side of the room to keep the wet edge fresh. This is especially important if you are using oil-based paint.*

Cutting in around door and window frames, skirtings and other edges may be done either before the main areas or between coats.

Two coats are usually sufficient but, if the colour change is great, more may be required. Don't worry about the patchy appearance of the wet paint; this will dissappear when the coat is dry. Shading is another matter. It is caused by greater thickness of paint on some areas than others. If shading is noticeable when the paint is quite dry, another coat is necessary, and you should avoid overlapping in the same places as in the previous coat.

Using a roller: The same procedure applies as for a brush. The main differenc is that all cutting in of edges and corners (where the roller won't

reach) is done first. Pour paint into the tray leaving half of the slope uncovered. Dip the roller in the paint and roll it on the slope until it is evenly charged.

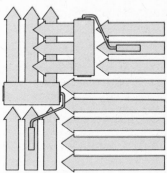

Roll the paint onto the wall in overlapping strokes about 30cm long and then change direction to cover the area completely. You will soon be able to judge how far to spread each roller full of paint.

Oil-based paint

Painting walls and ceilings with oil-based paint takes longer than with water-based as it takes more effort to spread it. However, it needs longer to dry. Each surface must be completed without stopping as it is not possible to overlap dry edges without showing brush marks. Do ensure good ventilation as the fumes are heavy. Use the undercoat recommended for the colour you intend to use. If the surface is porous, prime with undercoat thinned 10% with white spirit. If you are painting over wallpaper, remember that it will be difficult to remove the paper later. Two coats of top coat will be necessary.

In addition to new fittings, the transformation of this coldly lit bathroom is helped by the reflections and highlights in the gloss finish paint. Use moisture-resistant paint for damp rooms such as kitchens or bathrooms.

Interior Woodwork

Bare wood requires three separate layers—primer, undercoat and top coat. *Primer* soaks into the wood and takes up all its absorbency. This gives a uniform surface on which to apply the undercoat. *Undercoat* builds a thickness of a suitable colour on the surface and it also adheres well both to the primer and top coat. *Top coat* protects what is underneath. These are three different materials and are formulated to be used together.

New wood needs to be sanded smooth and sharp edges should be slightly rounded. Then remove the surface dust with a rag dampened with white spirit. Seal knots with shellac or proprietary knotting.

Primer should always be stirred first. Brush well in to the wood paying particular attention to end grain and any areas of greater absorbency. Allow to dry completely.

If you prefer, a water-based acrylic primer can be used, but the water will rise the grain of the wood, so the surface will not be smooth.

Undercoat should be stirred well. Use the colour that is recommended for the top coat you have chosen. Brush it on as heavily as possible without sagging or running. One coat is usually enough for interior wood, but for a better finish, apply two thin coats, rubbing down lightly after each one. Allow to dry completely.

Top coat should be stirred unless the instructions say otherwise. Oil-based paint doesn't brush on as quickly or as easily as water-based paint.

Use steady brush strokes to spread it evenly to avoid runs.

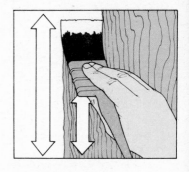

Brush on the top coat smoothly in the direction of the grain of the wood. Then go across the grain to evenly distribute the paint. Finish off with very light strokes with the grain again and towards the area just finished.

Old paintwork, if it is sound, only needs washing with a mild detergent solution and rinsing with water. Gloss must be rubbed down with fine abrasive paper or treated with liquid sander. Top coat may be applied directly unless you are changing the colour. In which case, undercoat should be used first.

If there is any flaking of the old paint, use a scraper to remove unsound areas. Then feather the edges of the surrounding paint with abrasive paper. When only sound paint remains, coat the areas of bare wood with primer and fill and paint as for new wood.

Windows

When painting next to the glass, always be sure to cover the join between the glass and the putty. Use a cutting-in brush and, if desired, a paint shield to keep the lines straight. Runs and splashes may be

Filling

Fill splits and dents with a resin filler using a flexible knife described earlier. For a superior finish, fill open grain and end grain. This is done by mixing the filler to a creamy consistency, spreading it across the grain of the wood, and then scraping the surplus away with the knife, leaving the filler in the grain. Do a small area at a time to be sure the filler doesn't set before you scrape it off.

When the filler is completely dry, smooth the entire surface with fine abrasive paper, being careful not to rub through the primer on corners. Remove the dust and apply a coat of primer over the filler.

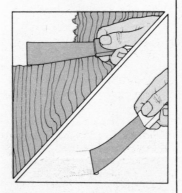

scraped off the glass when the paint is dry. There are scrapers made specifically for this purpose.

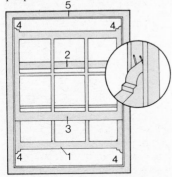

Sash windows should be painted in this order. Leave them open to dry, and insert matchsticks between the sashes and frame to prevent them from sticking together.

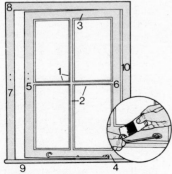

Casement windows are painted in this order. Leave the stay until last so you can adjust the window and hold it still without touching it.

Doors

Remove all fittings and wedge the door open. Use a narrow brush for mouldings and the edge of the door.

Flush doors should be painted in several horizontal strips,

30cm or so wide. Start at the top, brush the paint in all directions and then finish off with light upward strokes. Work quickly and blend each section with the strip above. A large brush is useful as it speeds the work and minimizes join marks in the paint. Use a small brush for the edges.

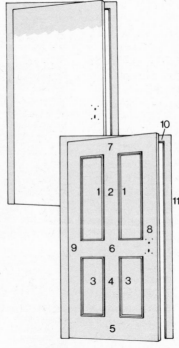

Panel doors are painted in this order. Paint the panels from the edge toward the centre of each. Extend the paint slightly over the rails (horizontals) and stiles (verticals) and finish off neatly along the joins to follow the grain of the wood.

Skirting boards

It is important to remove dust and hair from skirtings and the surrounding floor. Use a cutting-in brush for the join

with the wall and a larger brush for the rest, unless the boards are quite narrow. To protect the floor, you can use a piece of card or paint shield pressed into the corner between the skirting and floor, moving it along as you paint.

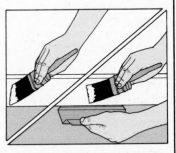

If there is carpet and you don't want to remove it, either use a cutting-in brush to get as near to it as possible, or use a paint shield. Wipe the shield clean of paint each time you move to another position.

Floors

Generally speaking, paints meant for walls and woodwork are not durable enough to be used on floors. However, a little-used room or the edges of partially carpeted stairs may be painted as for woodwork. It is important to remove any wax that may be present with white spirit and wire wool.

There are paints made specifically for wood or concrete floors. These should be used according to the manufacturers' instructions. Bear in mind that a finish can be no harder than the material beneath it, so painted wooden floors are likely to show dents and scratches. Epoxy floor paint gives good wear on concrete and tiled floors.

Furniture and Metal

Wooden furniture should be prepared and painted as for woodwork. Pay careful attention when filling and rubbing down to keep the surface smooth. Also apply the undercoat and top coat thinly, rubbing down lightly after all but the final coat.

Wicker and basket weave are best painted with an aerosol spray or aerosol-powered spray gun. Apply in very light 'mist' coats until sufficiently covered.

Aerosol touch-up paints from auto accessory shops come in a huge range of colours and are ideal if the area is small, but may prove expensive on a large project. You must remember that these paints are cellulose based and cannot be used over oil-based paint.

Metals require specific primers before they can be painted. Most paints may be applied to metal, once it is primed, but water-based paints should be avoided. Also, be sure to use a primer that is suitable for the top coat. The instructions on the can will advise you.

Radiators and hot water pipes should not be painted with water-based paints as they cannot withstand the heat without softening and, perhaps, crazing. Use either oil-based paint or one of the heat-resistant enamel paints designed for the purpose.

Rub down with fine paper or wet and dry and remove any loose paint. Any areas of bare metal should be primed with a suitable primer. Rub down patches of rust to remove as much loose rust as possible, and treat with a rust inhibitor. Choose one that also acts as a primer to save time. Once prepared and primed, use undercoat and top coat in the normal way. Do not clog up bleed valves.

If you are repainting sound paint, simply wash the surface and rub down to key the new paint. Undercoat isn't necessary unless you are changing the colour.

Brass and chrome can be lacquered to prevent tarnishing. If possible, it's best to use a clear polyurethane aerosol spray, but you can use a brush. Prepare the metal with a metal polish and then clean well with white spirit. Wipe thoroughly with a clean, dry cloth.

Top far left *This old wicker chair and new bedside table have been sprayed with sax blue automotive paint to match the wallpaper border.*

Top left *If you can't hide it, make a feature of it. An unsightly pipe becomes a bright pipe!*

Above *By using the same colour and finish paint, you can blend ugly pipes and fittings with the wall behind. The contrasting colour and texture of the fan help the illusion.*

Left *Give an old chest of drawers a new lease of life with bright colours or a mural of your own design.*

Far left *A working fireplace would be painted with heat proof stove enamel, but this unused one has been given a lift with the same emulsion used on the walls. The white gloss on the mantel has been extended into the hearth to complete the picture.*

Special Effects

Beyond painting rooms and furniture an even colour, there are many different effects that can be achieved with paint, Stencilling, antiqueing, dragging, spattering, marbling, wood graining, tromp l'oeil, and mural painting have all be practised by professionals for years.

While some techniques require a good deal of skill, there are many that anyone can use to add interest to decorating. Try experimenting with colour: paint the knobs on your green chest red; use contrasting colours on different panels of the same door; the possibilities are endless.

Above A modern white bathroom that has been individualised by a simple stencil. Kits of stencil plates, brushes, and full instructions are available from art shops. Artists' acrylic paints are useful for matching colours of fittings etc.

Top A bright red front door is quite a special effect, even without a cat! The easiest way to do this kind of design, is to trace a picture onto graph paper. Scale up to size and tape this onto the door with a sheet of carbon paper behind. Trace over the design and paint to the lines.

Above *The use of strong colours is stimulating for the children using this playroom. Also, DIY furniture benefits from the added flair of a well designed colour scheme. Notice the chalk board that has been inexpensively made using matt black oil based paint.*

Left *Glass paint is available in transparent colours. This can be used freehand or with a simple stencil. Another alternative is to paint each pane a different colour, although this will reduce the light significantly.*

Special Effects

Sponge stippling

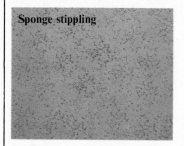

Bag graining

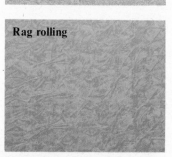

Rag rolling

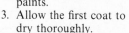

Four points to remember:
1. Choose paints that are suitable for the surface.
2. Don't mix incompatible paints.
3. Allow the first coat to dry thoroughly.
4. Practise the technique until you achieve a level of consistency.

Sponge stippling is suitable for water-based matt or silk finish paint. Paint the surface with the base colour and allow 24 hours to dry. Then apply one or more speckled 'glaze' coats by the following method.

Place a small amount of the glaze colour in a dish and dab the flat side of a slightly dampened natural (not synthetic) sponge in it.

Now gently dab it on paper until it leaves a delicate speckled print.

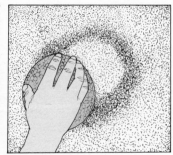

A cream base colour stippled with yellow, blue, and red.

Begin working on, for example, the wall until the pattern starts to grow fainter, and then recharge the sponge and dab it on the paper again before resuming. When this coat is finished, allow it to dry before applying any further coats. If you have made a mistake and sponged on too much paint in some places, this can be corrected by sponging on some of the base colour, after the glaze coat is dry.

Bag graining is suitable for water-based matt or silk finish paint. This effect is produced by brushing a glaze coat over a base coat and then using a rag-filled plastic bag to create a pattern that allows the base coat to show through.

Two people are necessary — one to brush on the glaze coat, and one to do the graining. When the base coat is completely dry, dilute the glaze colour 50/50 with water and stir well.

Using a large brush, one person should start painting the wall in vertical strips about 60cm wide, working from top to bottom. As soon as a small area is covered, the second person must lightly press the bag over the wet surface. This is done by placing and lifting the bag, without skidding, each time overlapping slightly the area just finished.

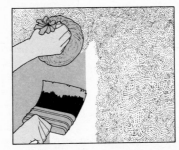

As one strip is finished, the first person must quickly begin the next, being careful not to overlap onto the previous one. Then, following closely behind, the second person should overlap slightly to keep the texture even. It is important to work quickly and not to stop until a wall is finished, as the graining cannot be done when the paint starts to dry. If the glaze coat seems to be getting darker, wipe the excess paint from the bag with a cloth. Be sure to mix enough glaze colour before starting.

Rag rolling is suitable for oil-based eggshell finish paint. This effect is achieved by brushing a glaze coat of oil-based eggshell, thinned 50/50 with white spirit, over a base colour.

Two people are necessary — one to brush the glaze colour, and one to rag roll it off. Brush on the glaze colour in 60cm wide vertical strips. As oil-based paint takes longer to dry than water-based paint, the person brushing on the glaze coat can work one or two strips ahead.

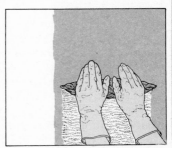

As soon as one strip is finished, fold a 30cm square rag into a sausage shape about 15cm long. Starting at the bottom, roll the rag up the wall, not allowing your fingers to touch the paint. (Wear rubber gloves to keep your hands clean.) When the rag becomes saturated, refold it and continue. When it's completely soaked, change to a fresh rag.

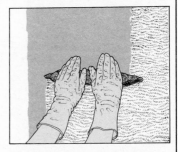

When the first strip is finished, begin at the bottom again and roll up a second strip, slightly overlapping the first. Leave 5cm or so unrolled at the edge of the strip of glaze, and brush on the second strip slightly overlapping the first. Begin rolling at the bottom as before, overlapping the edge of the two strips. Re-roll any areas where the glaze is too thick, and be sure to finish each wall without stopping. Rag roll some paint on to areas where the glaze is too thin.

EXTERIOR PAINTING

There are two main points to bear in mind when considering painting the outside of your home. One is that the main purpose of the paint is to protect what is constantly being attacked by the elements. Water, wind and sunlight will make short work of exposed wood and ferrous metal, so it is important to do the job properly and to keep outside paintwork in good condition. Secondly, the job is almost certainly larger than it looks. Walls that look small and accessible from the ground appear quite different from the top of a 6-metre high ladder.

As with interior painting, you should begin at the top and work down. It is usual to start with the gutters and eaves, followed by the walls, and the woodwork and drainpipes. However, if you are using scaffolding that is difficult to move, devise a plan that allows the maximum amount of work to be done on each section, before moving to the next.

With all exterior painting, the weather must be warm and dry. Rain, frost or condensation will spoil wet paint, so if the weather is doubtful, it is better not to start.

Begin with the side of the house that is warmed by the sun first. This will give the best chance of painting after the dew has evap-

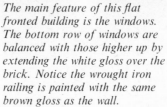

The beauty of this traditional timber cladding and trellis work is well worth the maintenance required. Micro porous paint is best for new wood.

The main feature of this flat fronted building is the windows. The bottom row of windows are balanced with those higher up by extending the white gloss over the brick. Notice the wrought iron railing is painted with the same brown gloss as the wall.

A dark colour around the bottom of the walls can help to hide the inevitable spattering of dirt that is thrown up when it rains.

orated. Continue around the house, following the sun, and stop painting at least two hours before sunset to prevent condensation settling on the wet paint. Remember that the surface of the wet paint will be slightly colder (because of evaporation) than the surrounding air, so avoid very humid days when condensation may be a problem.

Choose paint for masonry walls according to the texture you want to achieve. Oil-based paint must be gloss as it is more moisture resistant than eggshell finish. Emulsion is matt finish and the easiest to use, but not as durable as some of the water-based resin paints that contain mica chips. These *masonry paints* are available in thin emulsion-like liquids and also thick mixtures that give a stucco effect. However, it is worth noting that these are not as easy to apply as emulsion and are very hard on brushes.

If you are considering using micro porous paint, you must also use a micro porous primer. Remember there is no point in using it over old paint.

Finally, it is impossible to successfully paint damp materials. Any areas of recurring dampness should be investigated and the cause found and cured.

Preparing and Painting Walls

New masonry

Whether of brick, stone, concrete, cement rendering or pebbledash, this is prepared in the same way. Use a stiff brush to remove dust and loose material from the surface, and watch out for white crystals that may appear on damp areas. If you find any, wire brush them off and remember where they were, as you must check for their return for at least a week before painting. Keep brushing them away until the area is completely dry.

Treat *moss and mould* with a solution of household bleach mixed 1 part bleach to 4 of water. Brush it on generously and allow two days for the bleach to neutralize before painting.

Fill *cracks and holes* with a sand and cement rendering mix after brushing out loose material and wetting the area. Allow to dry.

Finally, *seal the whole surface* with a proprietary masonry stablizer. This will neutralize any alkali in the wall and ensure good adhesion of the paint. It also has the added advantage of making the first coat of paint go further because it makes the surface less absorbent.

Previously painted masonry

This is prepared according to the type of paint that was used before.

Oil-based paint is best washed and prepared with liquid sander, or you can use household detergent, remembering to rinse thoroughly and then rubbing down to key the new paint. On rough surfaces, rubbing down is impossible. Scrape off any loose paint and fill cracks with exterior-grade filler.

If the edges of bare areas are obvious, use filler to bring the level up to that of the sound paint. Finally, prime areas of filler with primer/sealer. If the texture of the filler is noticeable, brush undercoat on the repairs to blend them in.

Emulsioned walls should be washed with water as strong cleaners may damage the paint. When dry, fill with exterior-grade filler and seal the repaired areas with primer/sealer.

Cement-based paints are not washable and should be dry-brushed until a sound surface is reached. Repair faults and seal with masonry sealer.

Masonry paints are resin-based and contain granulated quartz or mica. Although water-based, they are waterproof when dry, and they tend to peel off rather than flake. Scrub with water and a stiff brush. Test corners and crevices with a scraper to make sure the paint is adhering well to the wall. Scrape off any loose areas and fill and prime as necessary.

Painting exterior walls

Having selected your paint, you may use a brush or roller.

For a roller, use a deep rectangular tray that hangs from a ladder or scaffold pole. This will carry more paint and you can load the roller with one hand and roll it up and down the inside vertical face of the tray.

A stiffer brush or long pile roller is best for rough surfaces.

Start painting at the top and work down in sections you can reach, trying to keep the wet line going. If possible, make the joins between sections where they will show least, i.e. along pipes or in line with windows. Try not to make the joins in exactly the same places on subsequent coats. Cut in around windows, edges and difficult places before painting the main area.

It is better to finish for the day having completed a wall rather than start another and leave it unfinished overnight. Apply the paint generously to keep the number of coats needed to a minimum.

Order of Painting:
1. Gutters and Eaves
2. Walls
3. Drainpipes
4. Windows and Doors

When choosing colour schemes for exteriors, the most important thing to consider is the environment. What looks right in one situation may not be suitable in another. Use of extreme colours or designs may be fun but could offend your neighbours – they see more of the outside of your house than you do.

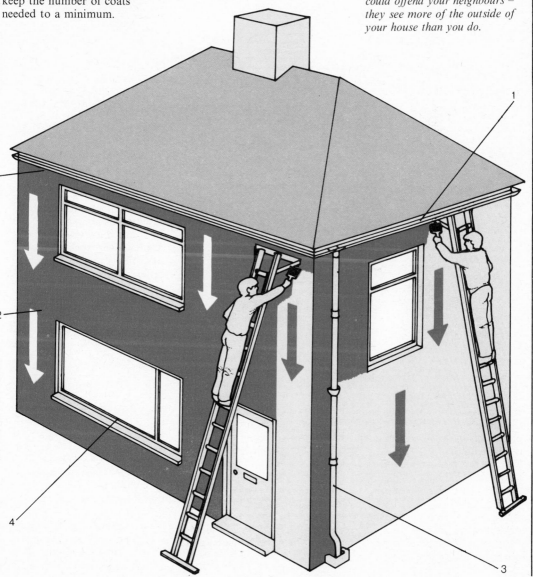

Woodwork and Metalwork

First assess the condition of the wood you intend to paint. It's possible that moisture may have penetrated and started to rot it, even though the paint on the surface appears sound.

Prod the wood in search of soft areas and uncover and dry out any sodden parts.

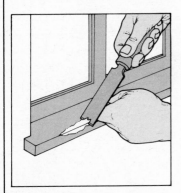

Rotten wood must be removed and the area treated with wood preservative. Choose one that can be painted over. Apply it liberally by brush and be sure to treat the entire area including the masonry and anywhere the rot may have penetrated. Also, scrape the paint away from the surrounding areas and treat these as well. Apply two coats and allow to dry thoroughly.

The surface must then be made good with exterior-grade filler or new wood, not forgetting to treat any new wood as well.

New wood should be sanded, and treated with wood preservative. Then prime with a primer that is compatible with the paint you intend to use (i.e. microporous etc.). Fill faults with an exterior-grade filler and prime the repairs.

Previously painted wood. Scrape off loose flaky paint, fill if necessary, and prime the repairs. Wash and rub down sound paint or treat with liquid sander.

Weather sealing. The next step (whether new or old wood) is to seal all the joins between pieces of wood, wood and masonry, and wood and glass. The best material for this is oil-based mastic, sold in cardboard tubes. It is completely waterproof and remains flexible enough to accommodate movement of the wood without breaking the seal. Primer should be applied before mastic (or putty). Careful sealing of all the joints will ensure the damage does not happen again.

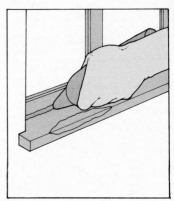

Squeeze mastic from the nozzle of the tube, working it well into the joins. Wipe off any excess with a cloth dampened with white spirit. Leave it for 24 hours to form a skin before painting.

Once prepared, primed and weather sealed, undercoat and paint as for interior wood. Apply at least two full top coats to everything; three are better.

On *wooden walls*, paint along as many boards as you can at a time, keeping the wet edge fresh to avoid join marks in the paint. Always work from the top downwards, whether the boards are horizontal or vertical.

Exterior metal

Metal window frames that have been painted before should have loose paint removed and be checked for signs of rust. If the paint is sound and there is no rust, wash and rub down with wet and dry and water, or treat with liquid sander. Rinse with clean water. Then undercoat and paint with gloss finish oil-based paint.

If there is rust, remove as much of it as possible with a wire brush. Treat the area with a *rust inhibitor*. Be sure to choose one that does not affect painted surfaces. When dry, wash and rub down sound paint or treat with liquid sander, and undercoat and paint as above.

New metal window frames should be already primed by the manufacturer. Clean them with white spirit on a cloth to remove any traces of oil or grease. Undercoat and paint as above.

Aluminium that has been painted before should have loose paint removed and the sound paint washed and rubbed down or treated with liquid sander. After rinsing and drying, prime bare areas with a primer suitable for aluminium (see advice on the can) and then undercoat and paint. One top coat is sufficient for aluminium, providing it is well applied.

Aluminium that has never been painted must be rubbed down with wet and dry and water with a little detergent. Rinse, dry, and prime with a suitable primer. Then undercoat and paint as above.

Gutters and drainpipes of steel or cast iron need good maintenance if they are to last. Remove loose paint and rust with a wire brush, and treat bare metal with a rust inhibitor. Wash and rub down sound paint, or use liquid sander and rinse. The inside of gutters should be painted with bitumen paint and the outside undercoated and painted with oil-based gloss.

Plastic drainpipes and guttering may be painted after washing and rubbing down with fine sandpaper to key the paint. Primer and undercoat are not necessary, nor is painting the inside of gutters. Remember that, once painted, they will need repainting regularly to keep their looks.

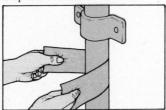

An easy way to rub down drainpipes is to wrap a sheet of wet and dry around the pipe and pull side to side.

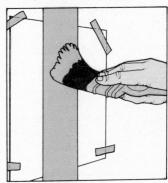

When painting drainpipes, hold a piece of card (or tape it to the wall) behind the pipe to keep the paint off the wall.

Wrought iron fences and railings are quite resistant to rust, but paint won't adhere to rusty areas. So it is necessary to remove loose paint and use a *rust converter*. This is a thin liquid that combines with rust and changes to a black colour. As it is thinner than a rust inhibitor, it is easier to apply to complex shapes. Use primer on bare areas and liquid sander on sound paint. Rinse and paint as usual. Don't be tempted to paint fences and railings with a spray as most of the paint will be wasted; use a brush and oil-based gloss paint.

Tips

If there is a large amount of wood and metal work to be painted, prepare only as much as you can prime in a day. Don't leave wood or metal bare to the weather.

TOP TEN TIPS

1 Estimating the amount of paint, primer, undercoat, etc. you need, is difficult to do accurately as rough surfaces require more paint than smooth ones. However, each can of paint has a guide to the coverage you can expect for each coat.

This is usually given as the number of square metres covered by each litre of paint. When you are buying the paint read the label of each can to see how many litres you need. Remember to allow this amount for each coat.

For oil-based paint on woodwork, one door takes about one-tenth of a litre for each coat. For windows, skirtings, etc., try to visualise the area compared with the door. Remember to allow for two coats.

To calculate the area of walls, multiply the length (L) of each wall (not forgetting alcoves or sides of chimney breasts, etc) by its height (H). Add the results together to give the total wall area. Subtract the area of windows, doors, etc not being painted, but don't forget gables, etc, for exterior walls. A room's ceiling area is usually equal to the floor area (multiply the room's length by its width).

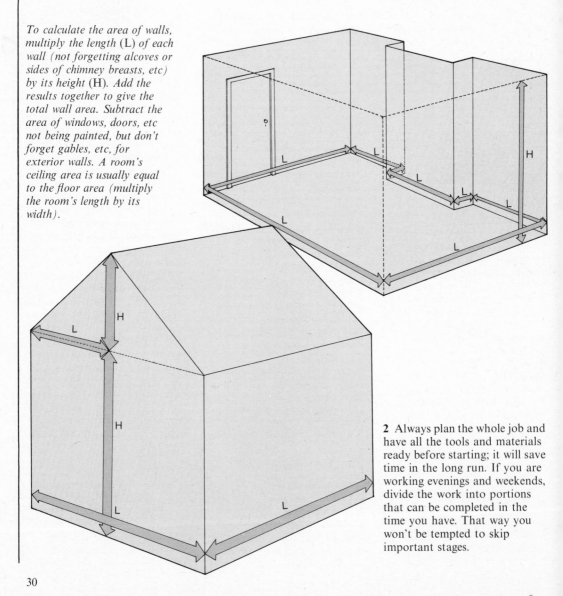

2 Always plan the whole job and have all the tools and materials ready before starting; it will save time in the long run. If you are working evenings and weekends, divide the work into portions that can be completed in the time you have. That way you won't be tempted to skip important stages.

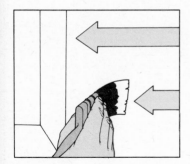

3 To prevent a ridge of paint building up on corners and edges, always brush or roll paint outwards over edges, never inwards.

For narrow edges, always use a small brush or a large brush edgeways on.

4 Cut in to corners neatly, holding the brush this way.

5 Drips in paint that is too dry to brush over can only be rubbed down with wet and dry when the paint is hard. Don't be tempted to overpaint runs and drips while they're tacky.

6 Oil-based paint takes several days to harden after drying. Leave shelves and window sills free of books and vases etc. to avoid marks in the paint.

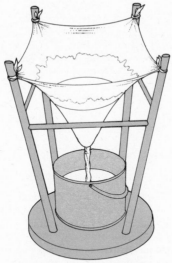

7 Old paint that is full of bits can be strained through nylon tights. Be sure to stir thoroughly first.

8 Don't use machines (electric sanders etc.) to rub down old exterior paint. Old primers may contain lead which is toxic and must not be inhaled.

9 To prevent a skin forming on top of paint that is going to be stored for some time, make sure the lid is on tight and store the tin upside down. Then, when the tin is opened later, the skin will be at the bottom and the fresh paint at the top.

10 To rescue an old tin of paint that has a thick skin on it and is full of dirt and hardened pieces of paint, don't cut the skin away. Instead, replace the lid and turn the can upside down and remove the bottom of the can with a can opener. Then you can pour (or scrape) out the useable paint.

Safety Tips

Don't leave ladders and scaffolding unattended where children may play on them.

Don't leave them outside where a burglar could use them. Take them down and chain and lock them to a railing or pipe.

Rags soaked in oil-based paint or thinners can be a fire risk. Dispose of them by burning or put them in a metal container with a tight fitting lid.

Cans of paint and other products contain safety warnings about first aid in case of accidents. Read them *before* you need them.

Turn off all electricity before removing switch covers and light fittings.

Be sure to use non toxic primers and paints where they may be chewed by small children or pets.

When using mechanical sanders, always wear goggles and a face mask.

Don't wear loose clothes or a tie while using power tools.

Author
Dek Messecar
Series Consultant Editor
Bob Tattersall
Design
Mike Rose and Bob Lamb
Picture Research
Ann Lyons
Illustrations
Rob Shone

Dek Messecar is a professional joiner who has had experience of
all aspects of DIY.

Bob Tattersall has been a DIY journalist for over 25 years and was
editor of *Homemaker* for 16 years. He now works as a freelance
journalist and broadcaster. Regular contact with the main DIY
manufacturers keeps him up-to-date on all new products and
developments. He has written many books on various aspects of
DIY and, while he is considered 'an expert', he prefers to think of
himself as a do-it-yourselfer who happens to be a journalist.

Picture Credits

Front cover: Paint courtesy of
Dulux; Tools courtesy of Stanley.
Page 2: Left, Clive Helm; Right,
Michael Crocket. Page 3: Courtesy
of Dulux Paints. Page 10: Courtesy
of Berger Paints. Page 11: Jerry
Tubby/Ken Lumsdale. Page 15:
Julian Nieman. Page 18: Top, Clive
Helm; Below, Spike Powell.
Page 19: Top left, EWA; Top right,
Spike Powell; Below, Jerry Tubby.
Page 20: Top, Jerry Tubby/Ken
Lumsdale; Below, Clive Helm/Juliet
Glynn Smith. Page 21: Top,
Michael Nicholson; Below, Jerry
Tubby. Page 22: Above, Courtesy
of Berger Paints; Below, Tim Street
Porter/Zandra Rhodes. Page 24:
Left, Anne Kelley; Right, David
Cripps. Page 25: Courtesy of
Berger Paints.

The Do It! Series was conceived, edited and designed by Elizabeth
Whiting & Associates and Rose & Lamb Design Partnership
© 1983 Elizabeth Whiting & Associates and Rose & Lamb Design
Partnership

First published 1983
9 8 7 6 5 4 3 2 1

Published by William Collins Sons & Co Ltd
London · Glasgow · Sydney · Auckland
Toronto · Johannesburg

ISBN 0 00 411895 2

Colour separations by
Hong Kong Graphic Arts Service Centre
Printed in Great Britain by
William Collins Sons & Co Ltd